BONNIE and her BRACE

Thank you to my parents Rick & Doreen Harvey who carried me through my scoliosis journey.

Written by Lisa Evangelos
Illustrated by Althea Botha

Hi, my name is Bonnie, I'm eleven and a half.

I like baseball and ballet,
    funny jokes and making crafts.

One day I bent over, and my teacher saw my back.

She wondered "should your shoulder blade be sticking out like that?"

My mom took me to the doctor, and they took a few x-rays.

They said I have scoliosis, which means my spine isn't quite straight.

Scoliosis
/skoh-lee-oh-sus/

The doctors used some fancy words,
at first, they sounded scary.

CERVICAL
the neck

THORACIC
the upper and middle

I wanted to share them with you,
so when you hear them you won't worry.

There are three sections of the spine, that the doctors like to say. It helps them describe where your curve is on display.

LUMBAR
the lower

Your curve is measured in degrees, kind of like the weather.

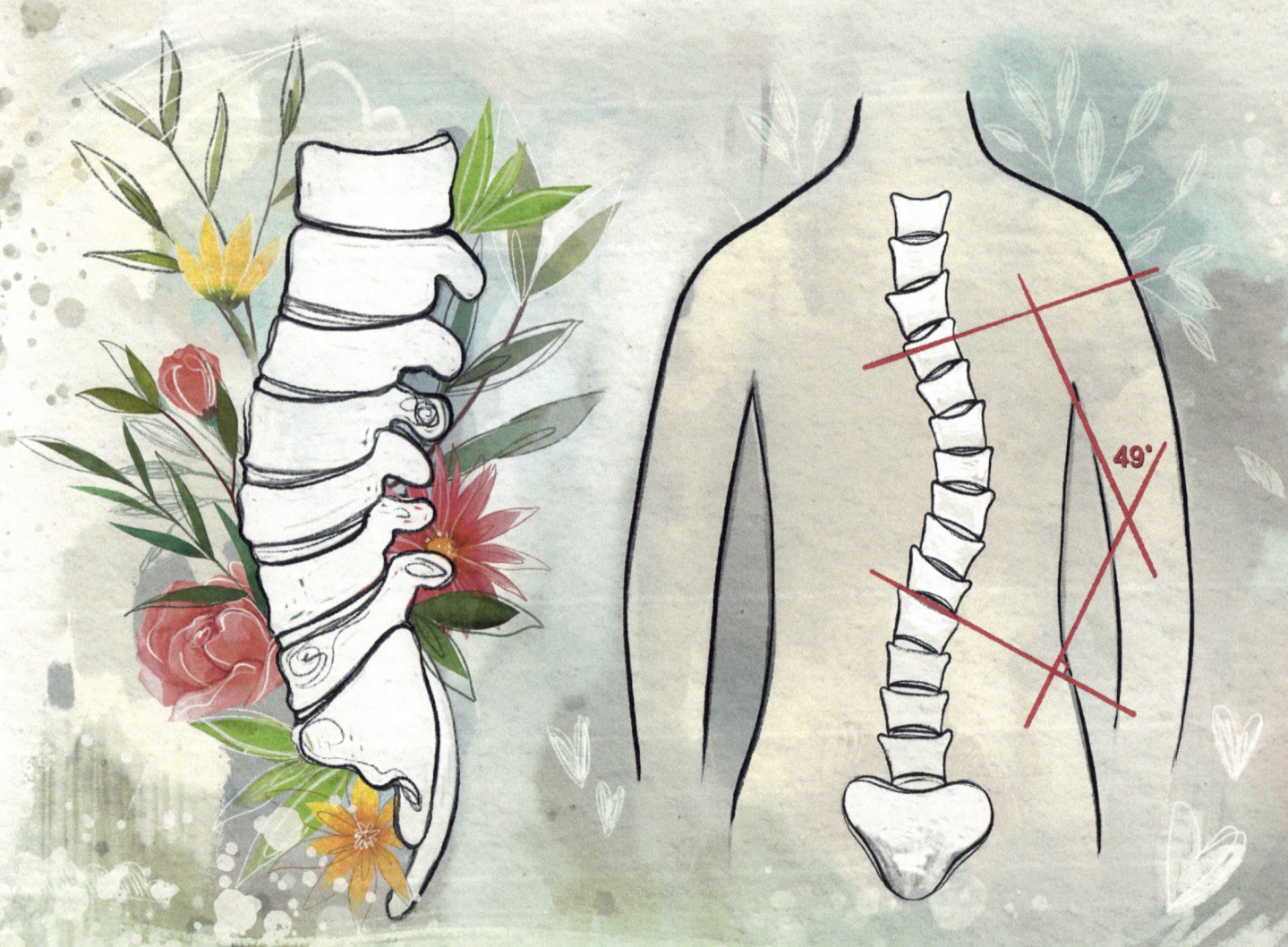

Sometimes there's only one curve, sometimes there's two together.

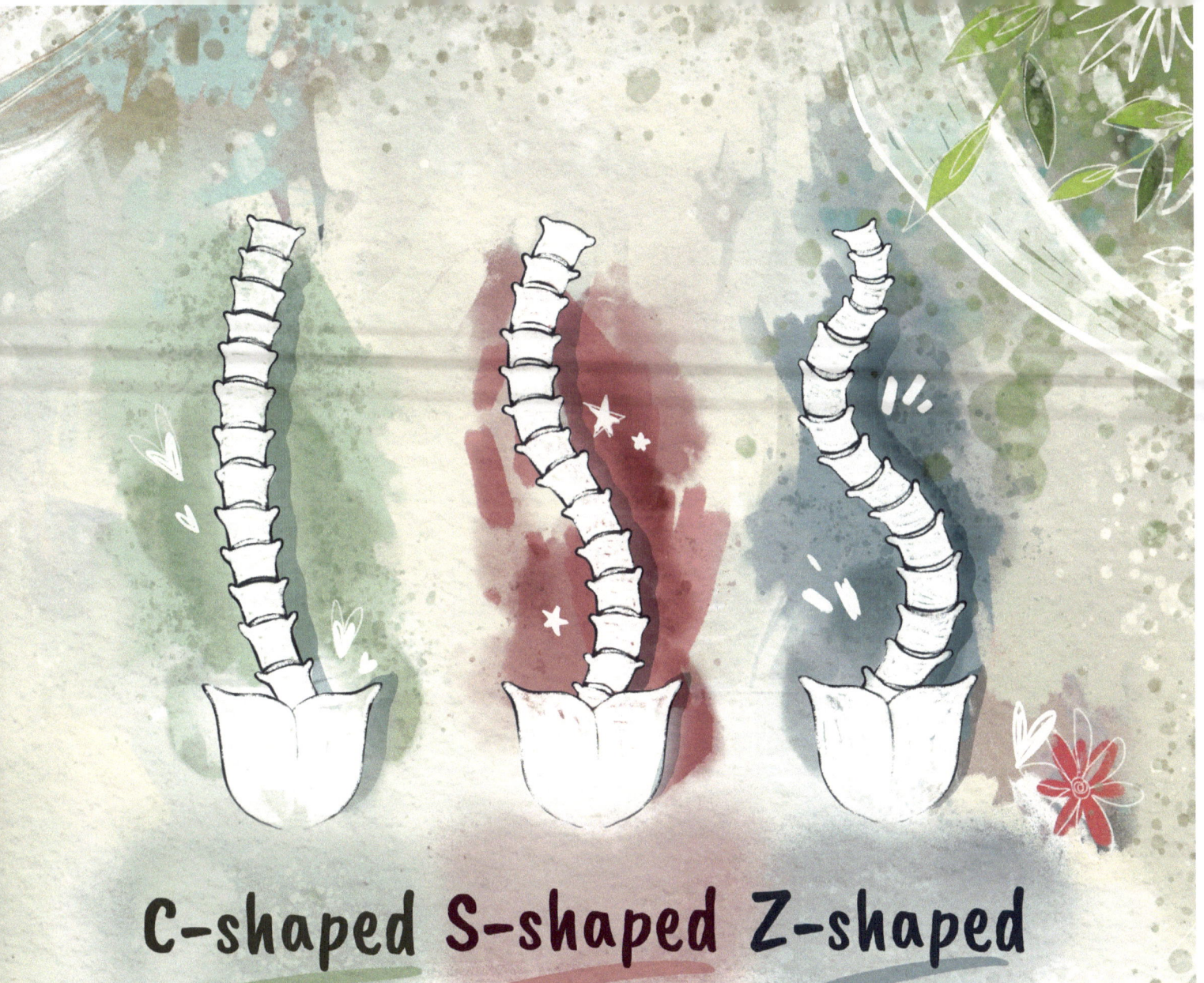

C-shaped S-shaped Z-shaped

In addition to the degree of curve, there's a letter that's assigned. You can have a C curve, an S curve or a Z curve in your spine.

Once you know your curvature in degrees and letter,

the doctor will prescribe a back brace to make it better.

There are a few different braces that the doctors like to use.

You can trust them to make the choice of which one is right for you.

You'll want to wear your back brace, as often as you can.

You can name it, decorate it,
have some fun with your new friend.

I named my brace Clyde and we are two peas in pod.

I take him everywhere I go and rarely take him off.

I hope you feel like now you know more about your diagnosis,

Clyde & I wish you all the best on your new journey with scoliosis.

For more information and support regarding scoliosis we suggest the following organizations:

THE NATIONAL SCOLIOSIS FOUNDATION
www.scoliosis.org

CURVY GIRLS
www.curvygirlsscoliosis.com

SCOLIOSIS ALBERTA
www.facebook.com/scoliosisalberta

Thank you so much to all my generous donors who made this little dream of a book come true:

Lindsey & Deb Lee
Tracey Silliker
Sarah Renner
Nadine Lennox
John Wort Hannam
Jeffrey Buck
Patrick Reilly
Dale Wilson
Rick & Deanna Showers
Erica Viegas
Loran Prince
Shweta Hanneman
Erin Schlepp
Valerie Evangelos
Doreen & Rick Harvey
Alison Naylor
Marian Vanderwal
Annelise Dyck
Kane Wolfe
Jocelyn Macaulay
Linda Miller
Jacqueline Foord
Marlen Walker
Rosalie Theberge
Geraldine Clark
Alissa Donaldson
Jen Gruninger
Leigh Acheson
Laura Svajlenko
The Blair Family
Arliss Sabine
Hugh Wakeham
Belle Hanneman
Chanda Bosch
Stephanie Stolk

www.ingramcontent.com/pod-product-compliance
Lightning Source LLC
Chambersburg PA
CBHW040024130526
44590CB00036B/83